The Colt from Old Regret

There was movement at the station,
for the word had passed around
That the colt from old Regret had got away ...
Banjo Paterson

The Colt from Old Regret

Dianne Wolfer & Erica Wagner

Colt gallops along a wallaby trail.
Crack! Stockwhips echo in the valley below.
Men are gathering at the homestead.

Tossing his mane, the colt from old Regret
tears through the scrub.
Stones clatter and crimson rosellas shriek
as he canters higher.

Colt rests by a creek. Alpine mint scents the air
and the icy water tastes of snow.
Brumby mares nicker in hidden meadows.
He answers their call, trotting closer ...

A stallion blocks his path.
Rearing, teeth bared,
Stallion screams a challenge.

Colt backs away,
but shadows the mob,
staying close when they
rest for the night.
White stars blaze
in the crystal air.

'Cooee!'
Daylight brings the sound of men.
The ranges ring with their snapping whips.

Colt hears the clink of bits and bridles.
Hooves pound up the mountain,
sparking firelight on flint stone.
Birds startle. He trembles.
The sky is a flurry of wings.

Colt smells saddles and tobacco.
He bolts, following Stallion's mob
as they canter through mimosa thickets.

Horsemen appear, whirling around the brumbies,
spurs glinting.
An old man, his hair white as frost,
circles the herd.

Another tosses a rope. Colt skitters and bucks.
The lasso falls to the ground.

Stallion gathers his mares, leading them into a gully.
Foals stretch lanky legs, nostrils flaring.
Colt runs with them, ever upward, snorting steam into crisp air.

The mountain's craggy brow is close.
Only one rider follows, a stripling of a lad,
his mare's flanks are bloodstained from the spurs.
Over the hills, Stripling chases the desperate mob.
Colt leaps wombat holes, his sides lathered in sweat.
Any slip is death.

The wild bush horses thunder across the mountain,
seeking shelter in a gorge.
Still Stripling hounds them.
His pony's hooves are sure and fleet.
Then he is amongst them, stockwhip snapping,
mountain pony heaving.

The brumbies stumble and halt.
Stripling rides between them,
and with a triumphant cheer, he turns the mob,
driving them back over the alpine meadows.

Other horsemen join him,
whistling and shouting,
'What a fearless ride!'
They muster Colt and the horses,
jostling them down steep gullies.

In the tamed land by the homestead,
the stockyard latch thuds into place.
A branding iron sears the air.
Colt smells burning flesh.

Mares huddle, sheltering foals.
Stallion rears in fury.
He circles his mob,
searching for a gap.
There's none.

A thin moon rises. Stockmen tend their campfires.
They fill their mugs and unroll swags.

In the darkness, Stallion snorts and paces.
His wild gaze meets Colt's.
They circle the yard, testing the fence.

With a defiant cry,
Stallion's mighty hoofs rise
up to split a beam.

Colt kicks aside the railing.
Brumbies push through
and charge towards the safety
of their beloved mountains.

Stripling's pony shies, snapping her halter.
She tosses her mane and gallops
beside the colt from old Regret.

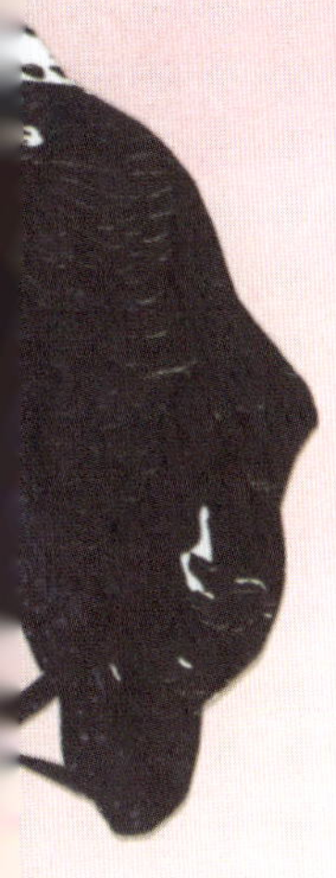

On the slopes of Kosciusko,
beyond human scent or sound,
Stallion's mob runs free of girth and reins.
In a higher, hidden valley,
where they never will be found,
Three horses graze,
sweet freedom in their veins.

The Man from Snowy River

A.B. 'Banjo' Paterson

There was movement at the station, for the word had passed around
That the colt from old Regret had got away,
And had joined the wild bush horses—he was worth a thousand pound,
So all the cracks had gathered to the fray.
All the tried and noted riders from the stations near and far
Had mustered at the homestead overnight,
For the bushmen love hard riding where the wild bush horses are,
And the stock-horse snuffs the battle with delight.

There was Harrison, who made his pile when Pardon won the cup,
The old man with his hair as white as snow;
But few could ride beside him when his blood was fairly up—
He would go wherever horse and man could go.
And Clancy of the Overflow came down to lend a hand,
No better horseman ever held the reins;
For never horse could throw him while the saddle-girths would stand,
He learnt to ride while droving on the plains.

And one was there, a stripling on a small and weedy beast,
He was something like a racehorse undersized,
With a touch of Timor pony—three parts thoroughbred at least—
And such as are by mountain horsemen prized.
He was hard and tough and wiry—just the sort that won't say die—
There was courage in his quick impatient tread;
And he bore the badge of gameness in his bright and fiery eye,
And the proud and lofty carriage of his head.

But still so slight and weedy, one would doubt his power to stay,
And the old man said, 'That horse will never do
For a long and tiring gallop—lad, you'd better stop away,
Those hills are far too rough for such as you.'
So he waited sad and wistful—only Clancy stood his friend—
'I think we ought to let him come,' he said;
'I warrant he'll be with us when he's wanted at the end,
For both his horse and he are mountain bred.'

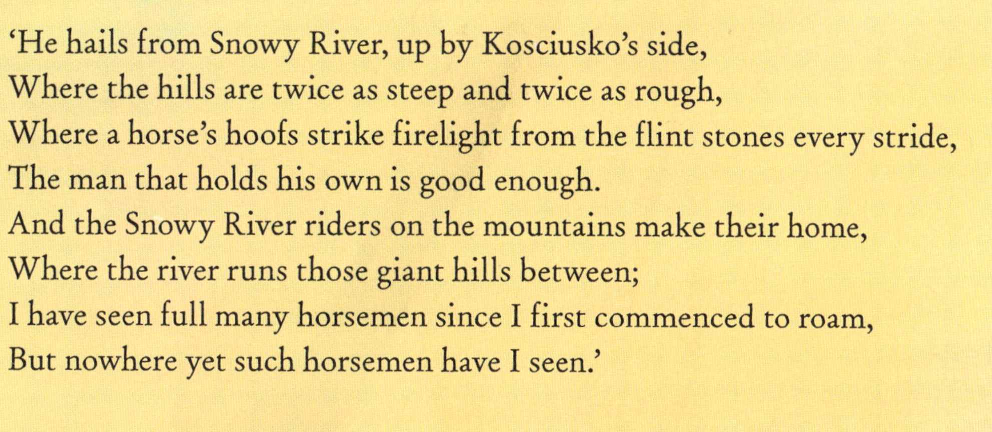

'He hails from Snowy River, up by Kosciusko's side,
Where the hills are twice as steep and twice as rough,
Where a horse's hoofs strike firelight from the flint stones every stride,
The man that holds his own is good enough.
And the Snowy River riders on the mountains make their home,
Where the river runs those giant hills between;
I have seen full many horsemen since I first commenced to roam,
But nowhere yet such horsemen have I seen.'

So he went—they found the horses by the big mimosa clump—
They raced away towards the mountain's brow,
And the old man gave his orders, 'Boys, go at them from the jump,
No use to try for fancy riding now.
And, Clancy, you must wheel them, try and wheel them to the right.
Ride boldly, lad, and never fear the spills,
For never yet was rider that could keep the mob in sight,
If once they gain the shelter of those hills.'

So Clancy rode to wheel them—he was racing on the wing
Where the best and boldest riders take their place,
And he raced his stock-horse past them, and he made the ranges ring
With the stockwhip, as he met them face to face.
Then they halted for a moment, while he swung the dreaded lash,
But they saw their well-loved mountain full in view,
And they charged beneath the stockwhip with a sharp and sudden dash,
And off into the mountain scrub they flew.

Then fast the horsemen followed, where the gorges deep and black
Resounded to the thunder of their tread,
And the stockwhips woke the echoes, and they fiercely answered back
From cliffs and crags that beetled overhead.
And upward, ever upward, the wild horses held their way,
Where mountain ash and kurrajong grew wide;
And the old man muttered fiercely, 'We may bid the mob good day,
No man can hold them down the other side.'

When they reached the mountain's summit, even Clancy took a pull,
It well might make the boldest hold their breath,
The wild hop scrub grew thickly, and the hidden ground was full
Of wombat holes, and any slip was death.
But the man from Snowy River let the pony have his head,
And he swung his stockwhip round and gave a cheer,
And he raced him down the mountain like a torrent down its bed,
While the others stood and watched in very fear.

He sent the flint stones flying, but the pony kept his feet,
He cleared the fallen timber in his stride,
And the man from Snowy River never shifted in his seat—
It was grand to see that mountain horseman ride.
Through the stringy barks and saplings, on the rough and broken ground,
Down the hillside at a racing pace he went;
And he never drew the bridle till he landed safe and sound,
At the bottom of that terrible descent.

He was right among the horses as they climbed the farther hill,
And the watchers on the mountain standing mute,
Saw him ply the stockwhip fiercely, he was right among them still,
As he raced across the clearing in pursuit.
Then they lost him for a moment, where two mountain gullies met
In the ranges, but a final glimpse reveals
On a dim and distant hillside the wild horses racing yet,
With the man from Snowy River at their heels.

And he ran them single-handed till their sides were white with foam,
He followed like a bloodhound on their track,
Till they halted cowed and beaten, then he turned their heads for home,
And alone and unassisted brought them back.
But his hardy mountain pony he could scarcely raise a trot,
He was blood from hip to shoulder from the spur;
But his pluck was still undaunted, and his courage fiery hot,
For never yet was mountain horse a cur.

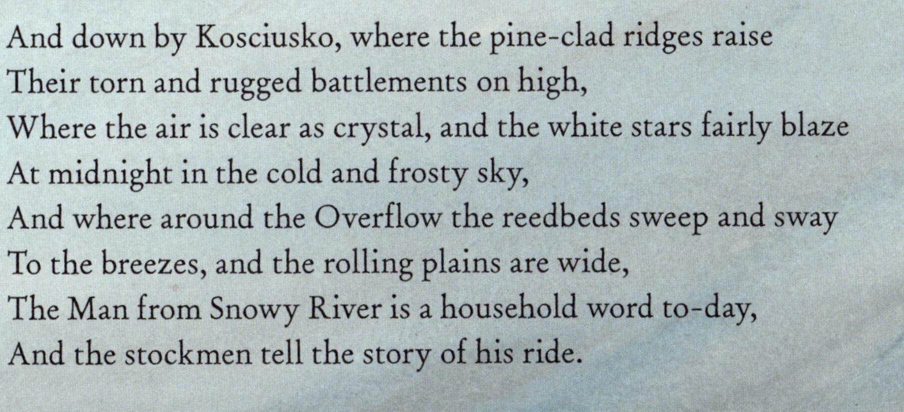

And down by Kosciusko, where the pine-clad ridges raise
Their torn and rugged battlements on high,
Where the air is clear as crystal, and the white stars fairly blaze
At midnight in the cold and frosty sky,
And where around the Overflow the reedbeds sweep and sway
To the breezes, and the rolling plains are wide,
The Man from Snowy River is a household word to-day,
And the stockmen tell the story of his ride.

Banjo Paterson

Andrew Barton Paterson (1864–1941) spent his early childhood on a farm in New South Wales, surrounded by emus, kangaroos and storytelling station-hands, including 'Jerry the Rhymer' who spoke in rhyme. He moved to Sydney at the age of 10 but held on to his love of the bush. He was working as a solicitor in the city, thanks to his family connections with the 'bush squattocracy', when he began to publish his poems in *The Bulletin.* Over the next decade, he became a regular *Bulletin* contributor using the pen name 'The Banjo', along with Henry Lawson and Norman Lindsay.

His poems were so popular that Angus & Robertson published a full collection in 1895: *The Man from Snowy River and Other Verses.* This volume generated classics of Australian poetry that celebrated bush life—including the poem that inspired this story—as well as humorous poems like *The Geebung Polo Club* and *Saltbush Bill.* It quickly sold a remarkable 7,000 copies, selling through its first print-run in a week.

The same year as *The Man from Snowy River and Other Verses* was released, Banjo heard a tune being played on the zither by Christina Macpherson and wrote a poem to go with it. The song was 'Waltzing Matilda'. The National Library of Australia holds one of Banjo's legal journals from 1892, which includes lines from famous poems as works in progress amongst his legal notes. 'You'll come a waltzing Australia with me' is crossed out and replaced with 'You'll come a waltzing Matilda with me'!

Banjo was a champion polo player, amateur jockey, lawyer, journalist and war correspondent. He served in the First World War, wrote scripts for broadcasting and performed storytelling and poetry. He is also one of Australia's best-loved poets, in print for 130 years.

Oh there once was a swagman camped in the billabong
Under the shade of a Coolibah tree
And he sang as he looked at the old billy boiling
Who'll come a waltzing Matilda with me
Who'll come a waltzing Matilda my darling
Who'll come a waltzing Matilda with me
Waltzing Matilda leading a water bag

Australian Bush Poetry

Traditionally, bush poems (also known as bush ballads) have a clear rhyming pattern. Poems are written in stanza form, usually with an Australian theme, relating to people living in remote communities and an outback way of life.

Banjo Paterson was a national celebrity in his day and popularised the now-iconic Australian figure of the bushman. Henry Lawson's works link to political and city themes, as well as the poignant hopes of bush folk, so beautifully expressed in *Andy's Gone with Cattle*. Female poets like Marie Pitts, Louisa Lawson (Henry's mother) and Dorothea Mackellar wrote about social justice, motherhood and love of country.

The Australian bush is the ever-present backdrop to the bush poets' stories. Natural elements recur in different poems by different poets: hills of granite, blazing suns, crystal-clear night air. Sometimes the bush is desolate and brooding, a place 'where beauty is not' according to Henry Lawson; and at others it is a thing of spectacular beauty, compared with gemstones by Dorothea Mackellar.

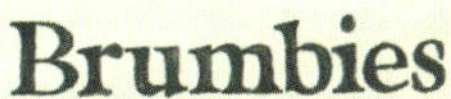

Brumbies

In 1788 seven horses arrived in Warrane / Sydney Cove with the First Fleet. Australian brumbies, or wild horses, are descended from the hardy animals that survived this voyage, as well as escaped horses belonging to early European settlers.

The name 'brumby' is thought to have come from Private James Brumby, a soldier with the New South Wales Corps in the late 1790s. When Brumby transferred to Van Diemen's Land (Tasmania), he let some of his horses run free. They were referred to as 'Brumby's horses'.

Present-day brumbies are versatile, hardy animals that have adapted well to our rugged bushland and challenging climate. They are renowned for their resilience, good temperament, sure-footedness and intelligence. Wild horses can be found in every state except Tasmania, surviving extreme desert heat as well as snowy alpine conditions. Over the years, other breeds, including draft, Arabian, thoroughbred and pony, have mixed with the original brumbies.

For many Australians, brumbies evoke a sense of freedom. They see these iconic horses as a heritage breed, one that is part of our history, reflecting the romance of the high country.

Equally, many Australians see brumbies as a feral pest that should be eradicated to protect high-country ecosystems, which are home to endangered species such as the corroboree frog and pygmy possum.

Who Was The Man from Snowy River?

Various people claim to know the identity of the stockman who inspired Banjo's fearless rider. Others believe Paterson created his character as an amalgam of different people.

Across the high country, there are hotels, pubs and parks named after The Man from Snowy River. The story is an especially important part of the history of the Upper Murray town of Corryong. In the main street, there is a life-size statue of the man and horse tackling the steep descent. Nearby is The Man from Snowy River Museum. And on a hill, in the town's cemetery, you can find the grave of Jack (or John) Riley, claimed by many to be The Man.

Jack migrated from Ireland to Australia as a thirteen-year-old in 1851. He loved the Snowy Mountains and became a legendary horseman, living for over thirty years in an isolated hut way up in the hills at Tom Groggin. Jack was a good mate of Walter Mitchell of Towong Station (father-in-law of Elyne Mitchell, the author of *The Silver Brumby*). Walter introduced Jack to Banjo. They hiked together and enjoyed many hours yarning around the campfire. Jack recounted the time he joined a group of stockmen who'd gathered to capture a wily thoroughbred stallion. When the horse raced down a terrifyingly steep slope, Jack gave a wild yell and followed. No-one expected him to survive. He did. And he singlehandedly corralled the escapee.

Other possibilities for the ballad's inspiration include Charles Lachlan McKeahnie, a fearless lad from Adaminaby. In 1895, when Charlie was still a seventeen-year-old 'stripling', he chased a valuable runaway stallion through rugged country near the headwaters of the Snowy River.

In his book *The Brumby Wars*, author and journalist Anthony Sharwood has another suggestion, arguing that the hero of Banjo's poem was an Indigenous stockman, a renowned horseman called Dick. When a mob of cattle got away, Dick chased them onto a spur, stopping just before a fearful descent. Richard Swain, a Wiradjuri man born and bred in the mountains, showed Sharwood a hill of granite and cypress pine in the Byadbo area. Sharwood writes, 'Nowhere else in the mountains or their adjacent flanks is there anything even remotely resembling pine-clad ridges'.

In 1988, historian Dr Bernard Barrett controversially quoted a story published in 1887 (three years before the publication of Banjo's poem) about another Indigenous rider, describing an 'exciting chase in which the horseman hero was a slightly built Aboriginal lad named Toby'. Ngarigo and Djiringanj man David Dixon told the *Bega District News* in 2018 that 'Banjo Paterson would not have been able to make a hero out of our people in his day'.

Author's Note

Family connections and a love of bush ballads sparked this story. Some of my earliest memories include my mother sharing her love of bush poetry with my sister and me. A country girl, she would often quote lines from *The Man from Snowy River* and *Clancy of the Overflow* (her two favourites), both written by Banjo Paterson.

Mum's stories of working in the shearing shed when she was young brought this era to life. Mum checked fleeces for dags, and was the tar girl, the one who ran to shearers when they accidentally nicked an animal. Smearing tar on a wound helped stop the bleeding so it was an important job. I was fascinated by the idea of a letter written by 'a thumb-nail dipped in tar', but I preferred the excitement and galloping rhythm of *The Man from Snowy River.* I could hear the crack of stockwhips, smell the dust and visualise all that 'movement at the station'.

Long ago, my forebears settled in the foothills of the Victorian alps. Further north, high in the Snowy Mountains, where stars shine bright at night, my sister and brother-in-law live off-grid on land adjoining Byadbo Wilderness area.

From one of my sister's lookouts, you can see a particularly ragged mountain cliff with a pine-clad ridge, said to be the only stand of pine in the area, and known locally as the place 'Where Dick took fright'. The story of Dick is an old one, about a young rider pausing at this fearful descent.

I often think of Banjo's words when I visit the high country, and one day some lines from his iconic ballad gave me pause:

But his hardy mountain pony
he could scarcely raise a trot,
He was blood from hip to shoulder
from the spur;
But his pluck was still undaunted,
and his courage fiery hot,

If the pony's 'pluck was still undaunted', I wondered, were those spurs necessary? I began imagining the poem from a different perspective, that of the horse.

The Colt from Old Regret grew slowly. I wanted the text to echo Banjo's beautiful words, without imitating his masterwork. In my version, the hardy mountain pony became a mare, a plucky companion for Colt. I wove carefully selected examples from *The Man from Snowy River* into my adaptation and hoped this creative re-telling would resonate with contemporary readers, as well as those who grew up loving the original poem.

The first read-through draft was dated mid-2019; shaping this 500-word story has been a long journey. I'm thrilled with the way Erica's magnificent illustrations have brought Colt's story to life.

For Mum, Karen and Owen, thank you for the bush ballads,
and for sharing your love of the high country–DW

For Craig, with gratitude for all the
adventures and those still to come–EW

Published by National Library of Australia Publishing
Canberra ACT 2600

ISBN: 9781922507686

The National Library of Australia acknowledges Australia's First Nations Peoples—the First Australians—as the Traditional Owners and Custodians of this land and gives respect to the Elders—past and present—and through them to all Australian Aboriginal and Torres Strait Islander people.

First Nations Peoples are advised this book contains depictions and names of deceased people, and content that may be considered culturally sensitive.

Publisher: Lauren Smith
Managing editor: Amelia Hartney
Designer: Hannah Janzen
Image coordinator: Madeleine Warburton
Printed in China by R.R. Donnelley on FSC®-certified paper.

Image captions: Thomas Rodolph Williams, *A Night in the Mount Barker Ranges*, c.1874, nla.cat-vn4935870; *Portrait of Andrew Barton 'Banjo' Paterson*, nla.cat-vn8047102; Page 56 in Andrew Barton 'Banjo' Paterson, *1892 Diary, Used as a Notebook* (detail), nla.cat-vn8047102; Jim Fitzpatrick, *Horseman Rounding up Brumbies in the Tumbarumba Mountains*, c.1960s, nla.cat-vn4589480; Jim Fitzpatrick, *George Day in the Australian Alps*, 1949, nla.cat-vn4589318; Karen Davidson, *Mountain Track*, supplied by the author.

Find out more about NLA Publishing at nla.gov.au/national-library-publishing.

A catalogue record for this book is available from the National Library of Australia